# HEAVY PENCIL

William Kempe, from *Nine Days Wonder* (1600)

# HEAVY PENCIL

## The Truth About Acting

by Dugald Bruce-Lockhart

ISBN-13: 978-1502566928

# CONTENTS

FOREWORD

Dear Reader,
Acting isn't rocket-science - we have all been storytellers at one time or another - but there are quite simply things to do and things not to do. This becomes particularly clear when performing in front of fifteen hundred paying audience members who may or may not share the same language or customs as yourself – as I found out on tour in Beijing, when I noticed an attractive blue lighting effect emanating from the audience while giving my St Crispin's Day speech as Henry V, only to realise to my stage-fright inducing chagrin that the blue lights were coming from a hundred or so not-so-strategically hidden i-phones and i-pads. (Chinese X Factor was on).

My twenty years of travelling the world with Propeller has taught me a great deal about the elusive art of acting and I owe much to Edward Hall and his unique gift as a director, storyteller and mentor. I now feel the urge to share what I have learned.

Much has been written about the art of acting and much of it is window dressing. There is only so much one can say about it before the waffle kicks in and the only thing left to do is get up there and do it. In the following few pages I offer all you need to know. The rest will be up to you.

Switch on the kettle, open that packet of biscuits, read this from cover to cover and then get out there and tell the story.

DBL, Barcelona 2014

**1**

## THE ACTOR

An athlete trains day in day out, year in year out, to be the fastest down the race-track. She puts in the hours, the pain and the sweat. She dedicates her total being towards being first across that line. If she trains hard enough she will be rewarded for her pains. She knows that raw talent alone is not enough – hard graft is everything.

Then comes the great day and she is ready. The athletes line up. The pistol shot echoes across the field and they set off. What a race! It's a foregone conclusion. She could not be that talented and that hard-working and not have won. All her friends know that.

As she crosses the line first it is not so much a surge of joy she feels, but one of relief. She's done it. It's all paid off. She was first across the line. She won. She won! As she turns to face the crowd she cannot stop a small tear from making its way down her flushed cheeks. Finally. After all the work. All the pain. She's done it.

But get this.

Moments later there's confusion. Panic. There's been a mistake. She hasn't won after all. Yes – she was first across the line but I'm afraid it doesn't count. She was wearing the wrong-coloured shorts.

## THE CRITIC

They're all set to go out for supper. He really fancies fish. Off they go to a nice little joint somewhere off the Strand near Covent Garden and they settle in for the night. But they don't have fish today. That's okay, he says – the menu still looks good and besides they both like the look of the wine-list and it's a top spot. Lovely atmosphere. They decide to stay.

And so instead he orders chicken. And so does she. By the time midnight rolls around they are the last to leave. The owner smiles and wishes them a good night.

They walk out onto the street and look for a cab. She is in raptures. The dinner was just wonderful! But something's wrong. He's not looking so sure. Is there a problem? No – there's no problem. It's about the chicken. Yes – he agrees it's the best chicken in London. Might even be the best chicken he's ever had. Trouble is he didn't want chicken. He really wanted fish. Sorry.

## THE AUDIENCE

She charges down the steps into the bar just as her best friend Jack looks up from reading the programme. A quick look around to see if anyone has noticed that she was the one they'd just been watching up there on stage. Yes – that guy definitely gave her a look. Wait – that's weird. He pulled funny face. Shit. What does that mean? In fact – where are the rest of the audience? That's the problem with the mid-week matinee. They all bugger off afterwards. She turns to Jack.

Jack is beaming. He congratulates her. She winces. It wasn't a bad show. Yeah – it was okay this afternoon, she supposes. Crap audience though. She says this to Jack. Jack is surprised and rather taken aback. He is suddenly in doubt. Maybe he didn't enjoy the show after all.

Meanwhile, in a car heading down the A3, an elderly couple who have also seen the show are chatting away as if their life depended on it. In the back seat is Beth's Grandson, Max. He appears to simply watch the world whiz by. But he's actually in a world of his own. He leaves the talking to the grown-ups. Now, these grown-ups have driven over two hours to get to the theatre today and they are unbelievably excited. They enjoyed it so much that they will tell all their friends and talk of little else for the next three weeks. In fact Beth, a keen member of the St Albans amateur dramatics society, has just decided to give Max a copy of the play for his ninth birthday. Five years later it is still his most treasured possession.

# 2

## TO ACT OR NOT TO ACT

Are you an actor?

Consider those awkward moments when new acquaintances pipe up at a dinner party. You're an actor! What – a real actor? Ever been on the telly? Are you in work at the moment? Let me guess – you're resting! I don't really go to the theatre, but have you ever done East-Enders? Sorry, I only watch Big Brother. A friend of mine got to the second round of X-Factor last year. Who's that guy in the film about Wimbledon? You know - that really good-looking guy. You should try and get into films. Do you know anybody famous? My mate says he saw Keira Knightley in Starbucks. Anyway - so how is it? I mean, you know – does it pay the bills?

Ah.

Here we go. If I get paid to do it – does that make me a real actor? On the one hand – yes it does. We all know the warm feeling we get when someone asks us if we are in work, and as luck should have it we have in fact just landed a job. What a relief! Ask me that again - but a little louder this time so that everyone at the table can hear. Yes. Suddenly I feel like an actor. I have just secured my rightful place at the dinner party. I'm sorry – did you just ask me if I was in work? Don't answer it yet. Enjoy the moment. Enjoy it. Am I in work? Actually I am, as it happens. Come on - appear casual. Sorry – you couldn't just top-up my wine? Thanks. Yeah – I'm about to start a six week stint at so and so... Yeah, I start rehearsals a week on Monday. Acting? Love it. Can't really imagine doing anything else actually. Yep. That's me. For my sins. I am an actor.

Everyone laughs with interested approval. Suddenly you are the centre of attention. But the centre of attention is not always the best place to be.

Right at that moment the guy sitting opposite who works for a law firm off Old Street asks – so, what's the money like for a gig like that?

The table falls quiet and everyone – including the cute guy at the end of the table who poured your first Gin & Tonic when you were all milling about in the kitchen earlier, and who also flirtatiously suggested he'd never been to an opera before but would be keen to give it a try under the guidance of someone creative but in control of their life – is suddenly smiling at you and awaiting your answer.

You have several options.

It's unlikely to be the one where you admit to a table of thirty-something career-types on generous five-figured salaries that you have agreed to put in six eight-hour days a week, for under thirty quid a day. (And that's pre-tax, pre-NI contributions, let alone the fact that your agent is fully within their rights to take their ten per-cent off the top – oh, and that your travel expenses will be at least £175 for the month for which, unfortunately you will not be compensated.)

As it is, you have already taken one for the team when you admitted to the table the finer details of your last job – where you dressed up as a blackcurrant-flavoured can of Tango and paraded up and down Oxford Street shouting "Free the rainbow of fruit flavours" for the tidy sum of £65. Which you will receive in over a month's time. And yes – that's minus tax, NI, and the agent's commission. (And no, they didn't pay your travel card.)

Which brings me to the implicit, yet much more real and sinister question within the original question:

Are you a 'successful' actor?

Well. You cannot stop another person's mind from judging. You cannot possibly think what they are thinking. You cannot with absolute certainty predict what people will do, or what they want, let alone what they think. You cannot change someone's mind. Only they can do that.

What somebody else thinks is not your concern.

But I repeat - are you a successful actor?

Well, I have gone to bed that night with a feeling that I belong in the world - that I have made a difference, a contribution. The pleasure and distraction of the day's events has for a moment stopped me worrying about things that can't be changed in the future. Instead allowed me to spend a little more time noticing the trees on the way home and how the falling leaves caught the late autumn light. The smell of wood smoke. The way the lone cloud had the same shape of a pond I used to play in with our next-door neighbour when my brother and

I were children. And those tiny minnows he caught with that old, broken green net.

But surely a successful actor is one that makes a living out of acting?

Not necessarily. An actor who makes a living out of acting is an actor who makes a living out of acting. In the same way that a Chemist who makes a living out of being a chemist is someone who makes a living as a chemist.

Some actors are lucky enough to support themselves entirely on acting work. Most do not. They have other means of income – or partners who help subsidise their incomes. The truth is that of the entire acting community, 95% of them are currently out of work. Whereas a chemist will work throughout the year with perhaps five weeks off for holiday, the actor may well have most of the year off and only get to work for twenty-eight days in total. This is simply due to the high proportion of actors and the scarcity of available acting work. It is not a criteria by which one can be judged successful or not.

But does that mean that if I have worked only ten days this year as an actor that I'm a success? Surely the plan is to get up there – up with the best – to get to the top?

Be warned.

If you're so concerned about reaching the top that you miss the view then it would seem you have missed the point of climbing up there in the first place.

The successful actor is the one who enjoys the view.

There is no other reason to be here.

# 3

## THE THRILLER

The audience settle into their seats as the house lights go down. The music swells as the lights come up on stage revealing a lone-standing bench, centre stage. The stage lights resolve and the music fades out. The stage is empty apart from the bench. The auditorium falls deathly quiet. The anticipation is total. They wait. Not a movement on stage. You can cut the tension.

And there you have it – dramatic tension. They are gripped. So far the play is working a treat.

Why?

Because right now the entire audience is thinking, 'What is going to happen next?'

As long as the audience are wondering what is going to happen next we are winning. We are telling the story in a successful way. The trouble is that sooner or later in a play the audience will start to drift, they start to anticipate or get ahead of the action, the attention will waver and they start to tune out of the scene they are watching and hope a better scene might follow – they hope that something just might happen. Worst case scenario – for the actors at least – the audience member will get up and walk out.

So what are the things that stop an audience from wondering what will happen next?

Before answering that directly let's think about that old actors' adage, 'Never work with animals or children.' The adage is indeed good advice – or a sound warning at least. For the minute an animal comes on stage, or a small child, we can't take our eyes off it. The actors on stage can forget about getting any kind of focus or attention until the animal or child leaves.

Why?

Because on seeing a small child or animal on stage the audience's immediate and unescapable reaction is to wonder what is going to happen next.

The fact is that for a whole host of reasons – not all of them being their own fault, as such - actors can very quickly become predictable. With an animal or small child, you can never, ever be sure of what they will do next. They are totally unpredictable. And this makes them riveting to watch. All storytellers - actors and directors - would kill to be able to deliver such dramatic tension for the entire length of a play.

There are some actors that get close to this – (we like to call them 'dangerous actors') but it is rarely sustainable for an entire play. As I mentioned before this is not necessarily all the actor's responsibility. The director may not have worked out the rhythms of the piece in the best way to help the story, or they may have failed to fully understand the story – meaning the audience won't either, even if the actors think they do. After all, how can you be expected to wonder what is going to happen next if you haven't understood exactly what has just happened before or happening right now? Also the actor may have mannerisms that soon telegraph what they are about to do or say... they may not be thinking 'on the line' (this will be addressed later), the lighting might not be helping at this point in the story...and of course the audience may well be so familiar with the story or even the very lines the actors are speaking that even this can work against us.

There are a hundred pitfalls to stop the audience wondering what will happen next. As storytellers this factor should be our main concern. A successful night out at the theatre is guaranteed if we can make this happen. Unfortunately the focus often appears to be on other areas – a common error being the theatre producers' misguided belief that a famous name and an expensive set will do the trick.

We have to keep the audience in their seats.

We have to keep them wondering what is going to happen next.

We have to tell the story.

**4**

## STORYTELLING. TEN TIPS

Don't play emotion. I am not interested in how your character feels, I'm interested in what he is going to do about it. This attempt to change the needs and beliefs in oneself, or someone else is what keeps the story alive and the audience in their seat. The attempts are also known as actions. Actions are good – actions develop a story. Emotions are states of being - states of being don't necessitate a response from another character. Emotions are by-products of actions played. Emotions don't develop the story. Actions do.

Play the positive. If you want somebody to do something for you, the best way to achieve this is to ask them nicely. Same thing applies to actions and text. Put a positive spin on everything you say, even the apparently negative thoughts, and you will open a door and invite a response. An open door keeps the scene alive, it allows room for growth and change. It keeps the audience in their seats. Close the door and the scene is dead, you are treading water and we find ourselves waiting for the next thing to happen. All scenes are a confrontation of ideas, (including soliloquys) where an attempt is made, however slight, to produce a better outcome. Play the positive and the scene will work, the story will live and the audience will want to know what happens next. The worst offence an actor can make is to play anger and indignation. Unfortunately, playing anger and indignation is often the actor's default position and it is the surest way to kill a scene dead. Whenever you can, no matter how extremely confrontational a scene may appear, find ways of playing the positive.

Don't waste time trying to 'find your character'. You cannot play character any more than you can play your name. Character is an outside perception by the audience resulting from what you do or don't do and what you say or don't say (your actions). What you do or don't do and what you say or don't say is governed by the text. The text is your character. If you can't 'find your character' then you are either not looking at the text, or you may need reading-glasses. Study the text and work out the situation. Play the situation and you get the character for free.

Think on the line. Don't act first then speak – the speaking is the thinking. Those little exhalations of breath, those grunts and sighs before you speak your line (which many actors feel is making their performance more 'natural') only advertise what you're about to say and make the words redundant. If you do that the audience will get ahead. Once the audience gets ahead of you the play is doomed, no matter how well you may think you are acting. The reason the audience stay in their seat is because they want to know what happens next or how it happens. The minute they get ahead they will start thinking about how they are going to get home after the show. All plays are ultimately exercises in suspense. Think on the line and the audience will never get ahead.

Don't play the punctuation. It is merely a written guide to aid comprehension when reading. It helps give structure to the length and meaning of a given thought. It sorts out parentheses and sub clauses for the reader. It is grammar. It is of no interest to the actor and the spoken word. There is nothing as criminal as a comma which for some reason tempts the actor to make unnecessary pauses just to obey the dots. Forget it. The only punctuation worth considering – but not necessarily playing – is the full-stop. A full stop marks the end of a thought and the beginning of a new one. And yet even here it doesn't mean we have to stop talking. Often there will be a full-stop half way through a line in Shakespeare. It is done on purpose. In order not to break the rhythm of the line we are forced to make a rapid thought change without breaking stride. This rapid thought change gives us insight into the state of mind of the person speaking and delivers that elusive and much sought by-product, 'character.' Such mercurial changes of thought are a great joy for an actor to play and thrilling for an audience to witness.

Don't get bogged down with research. Research can be useful to an extent - it may inspire and help the imagination - but it cannot be acted. You cannot play your deep 'character research'. What your character 'had for breakfast' will not help the scene on stage any more than knowing what your character's favourite colour is. At best research can be a tool which allows the actor to feel confident enough to let go of everything on stage and simply listen and react according to the demands of the script. At worst it is a lot of ultimately useless information that can stop the actor being present in the room. The text is your research. The more you explore the text the better the scene will be. A good driver can negotiate a racetrack instinctively but the more efficient driver will be the one who studies the track in minute detail first and then applies their instinct - the text is your race track. The text is your map. Don't leave it behind.

Don't let your acting process, your 'method', close you off to the other actors around you. Acting processes can be dangerous as the focus is all about yourself, your physicality, voice, Laban efforts etc. The most helpful tool you have is the other actor on stage with you. Look after them and your own needs will be taken care of. Without them and your relationship with them there will be no play, no story and certainly no character.

Learn your lines before you come to rehearsal. Actors will claim that they don't like to learn the lines in advance because they don't want to make judgements and pre-empt choices. They want to be 'free' and open in rehearsal. Which is odd considering they will have only four weeks in which to make these choices, (all of which are intrinsically bound up in the text) one week of which will be spent doing the actor's favourite pastime – sitting safely around a table discussing their 'character' and drinking endless cups of tea.) The fact is that the storytelling can only ever begin when the actors get on their feet. And the best rehearsal begins when the actors can look each other in the eye and actually listen to each other rather than hide behind a convenient script. The sooner you put the book down, the sooner you start telling the story. It's all about throwing paint at the walls. Some of it will stick, some of it won't. You can't throw paint if the lid is still on the tin. And rehearsal is no place to waste time choosing the colours you want. Do the work at home then come into rehearsal, take the lid off the tin and start throwing paint.

Don't blame the audience. There is no play without an audience. There is no such thing as a 'bad' audience any more than there is 'bad' weather. The audience will behave as it wishes, just like the weather – all the actor has to do is make sure it's 'wearing the appropriate clothing' and deal with it. This translates as sticking to the one thing that you are in possession of – the story – and forgetting about trying to second guess what the audience is thinking or why they aren't laughing. You will never know what they are thinking, or how much they are enjoying it or not. And the fact is you can't hear a smile. So relax and get on with your storytelling. If after your honest efforts the audience doesn't like what it sees then there is nothing more to be done – you can't persuade someone to want chicken if they'd really prefer fish.

Be bold. It's a play – so play! Don't be afraid of getting it wrong. What's the worst can happen? Everyone forgets lines, everyone gets moments of panic and self-consciousness. This a hazard of being a human being, not an automaton. The best batsmen have been out for a duck. World class skiers will continue to fall over. But the fact is...

...no one remembers a double-fault if it's followed by an ace.

**5**

SHAKESPEARE


Text-based theatre is ultimately a war of ideas where words and phrases are used as weapons to change another character's mind. The by-product of this war of ideas is the simultaneous development of story and also what we term 'character' (that elusive thing I mentioned earlier that actors claim they can never find.)

Think of thought as 'black and white', and think of emotion as 'colour'. We need to act in black and white, and let the audience experience the colour. And the sharper our black and white, the sharper and clearer the thought, the more colourful the audience's experience. The purer the thought, the clearer the perception of 'character' will be for the audience.

Actions are defined by thoughts and thoughts are defined by words. As soon as you add verse into the mix, rhyming couplets, alliteration and assonance, lyrical imagery, punning and verbal repetition, all of which might be crammed into a thought which is over five lines long (without a full stop – commas don't count) then the skill of playing actions is put to the highest test, for which the actor reaps the highest rewards.

And in this arena Shakespeare is king.

<u>Words and Phrases</u>

The way we stress words and phrase our thoughts is vital to understanding any sentence, let alone a line of verse. If we overstress words in a sentence then we may hear the individual words, but we won't understand what the person is trying to say. If we under-stress or stress the wrong words the same thing happens. The same principle applies to musical notes in a phrase of music - think of a song you know well and try singing it where you stress the wrong notes – it becomes clear instantly that something is wrong. The song basically disappears. And in terms of sentences – the thought disappears. And if we lose the thought then we lose the story. Ultimately verse is not about flowery speech and poetry, it is about clarity.

You will hear people say of a Shakespeare play (or any play for that matter) 'That was a really clear production.' Actors sometimes worry about this. Our insecurities kick in. Did they mean it was simplistic, too easy, not subtle enough, over-acted or boring or conventional? No. It means they mean they understood it. And oddly enough if an audience understands a story they are much more likely to enjoy it.

Shakespeare writes in blank verse and prose. The verse will sometimes rhyme – or indeed be composed of rhyming couplets – but more often than not the basic verse structure is simply blank verse, also known as iambic pentameter. To break that down, that means the lines are composed of iambs. An iamb is a two-syllable beat. It has a 'ti-dum' rhythm. Like the human heart. The 'dum' is the stressed syllable. The 'ti' is the unstressed. If you stick five iambs in a row you have an iambic pentameter. (Taken from the Greek, 'Pende', meaning five. Of course most of you know this - but for those of you who don't, knowing the clever terms for all this stuff will not make you a better actor but it always helps to be in the picture.)

So, the iambic pentameter:

"If *mu*sic *be* the *food* of *love*, play *on*"
(The italics indicates the stressed syllable, the 'dums'.)

Modern speech falls into a similar pattern:

A: I *really* don't a*gree* with *what* you *said.*
B: You *don't?*
A:              I *don't.* I *think* you *got* it *wrong.*

29

The basic principle is to stress the 'dums' (the bits in italics) and you won't go far wrong. It's also quite simply the most natural and obvious way to stress the line anyway. Try it. Try stressing the 'ti's' and you'll see. You will also find you will have put a slightly heavier stress on the final syllable, the final 'dum.' This is a good instinct. Because marking the last word of our thought helps other people know we've finished making our point – and they could now speak if they wanted to.

<u>Drive to the end of the line.</u>

As a general rule, in any written - or for that matter, spoken text - to aid comprehension (to gain that dreaded 'clarity') it always helps to drive on through 'til the end of a thought. Breaking up the thought simply doesn't help. The same applies to the Shakespearean line of verse. Drive to the end of the line and don't break up the rhythm of the line in an attempt to be naturalistic and make it sound like modern speech. Much like a phrase of music.

There is a sequence of notes, a rhythm and a tempo. If you mess with the flow, break the rhythm or change tempo half way through then the tune warps and becomes disjointed and at worst unrecognisable. So, set a tempo and drive to the end of the line. Don't stop or try to add colour to the phrase along the way. Shakespeare has done the work already – you just need to deliver what he intended and not interfere!

If music be the food of love, play on.

If (*what?*) If music (if music *what?*) If music be (if music be *what?*) If music be the (if music be the *what?*) If music be the food (if music be the food *what?*) If music be the food of (if music be the food of *what?*) If music be the food of love (if music be the food of love *what?*) If music be the food of love play (if music be the food of love play *what?*) If music be the food of love play <u>on</u>. (Ah – now I get it!)

When we do this we 'land' the thought. Aside of emoting, the next most common offence we actors make is to rush and not land the thoughts. If you don't land the thought the action becomes fuzzy and then so will the story and then along with that, so will your 'character'. Land the thought.

Sometimes a thought is as brief as one line in length but more often than not the thought will extend over several lines – perhaps as many as ten. As 21st Century folk we are used to speaking in sound bites – we live in a world of twitter and texts - and therefore aren't used to dealing with, let alone speaking, long sentences. It will take a lot of breath. And that will take some practice.

Does this mean you should do a ten-line thought in one massive breath? Perhaps. Great if you can. Unlikely though. Three to five lines should be doable, although it's distinctly harder when you're rushing up and down the stage waving a broad-sword. But don't worry because, as it happens, Shakespeare has provided a way of helping the actor on his way and given him a gift:

The line-ending.

We can use the end of a line to take a snatch breath to help us get to the end of a long, or complex thought. The blank verse is written with precisely that intention in mind. If you have to pause to take breath, the place to do it is at the end of the line.

This device is known as 'end-stopping.'

And it has its traps.

End-stopping is fine provided you use that mini suspension like a spring board to drive on through into the next line and onwards (i.e. maintaining the through-line of the thought.) It is bad when the actor simply marks the end of the line without the intent of moving forwards through the thought. A series of end–stops in this manner will start to sound like clunky nursery-rhyme but worst of all, the sense will be lost. Lose the sense of the line and you lose the story. Lose the story and you lose the audience.

The fact is, a thought expressed is only fully comprehended when completed. Which means if you dilly dally on your way with a long thought and don't drive to make your point, you will lose the comprehension along the way. Also known as waffle. (Add in the rich and lyrical imagery and metaphors that Shakespeare is inclined to use and you have a potential car-crash on your hands.) Unlike many modern writers Shakespeare doesn't deal in waffle, he gets to the point. He gets to the point with such economy that we start to use unhelpful terms like 'poetry.'

So – how do you stress a Shakespearean line of verse? You follow the rhythm and drive to the end of the line. If the thought is more than one line long then use the line-endings to propel you through towards the end of the thought.

This doesn't just apply to Shakespeare it applies to all text. Drive to the end of the thought and you are winning.

### Subtext

Ah.

Actors will often claim they simply aren't able to say a line until they know why they're saying it. Fair enough. But then again, how can you know what you're trying to say until you've said it?

The fact is the author has given you the line to say – there's no way around it. You're going to have to say it, like it or not.

You have two options. First is to ask thousands of interesting and tea-break-demanding tricky questions which allow everyone to look like conscientious and serious artists (including the assistant director, who can now show just how much research on Wikipedia they've done) and the second option is to put all thoughts of Stanislavski aside, take a deep breath, look your fellow actor in the eye, deliver the line and let the line inform you.

The actor should serve the text, not vice versa.

So - get out there and enjoy it. Don't act, don't show us how you feel, show us what you're going to do about it.

Let the words do the talking.

## A FINAL THOUGHT

There are two ways of making a statue of a dinosaur. One is to take a lump of clay and attempt to mould it into shape, bit by bit. The other way is to start with a large block of clay and chip away everything that doesn't look like dinosaur.

Strip away the peripheries of 'acting' and you are left with the story, the war of words, the thoughts. You are left with the text. The dinosaur.

The text is your dinosaur and it has already been created.

All you have to do is reveal it.

Printed in Great Britain
by Amazon.co.uk, Ltd.,
Marston Gate.